Omega Mountain

Finding God's Comfort & Peace After A Loved One Transitions To The Next Life

By Dario Thomas [Copyright January 1, 2019]

Table of Contents

Lord Let Him Live!!!

This was my persistent prayer; it had become my mantra for a number of months. I found out that my brother was terminally ill. I couldn't believe it! He was too young to die! This can't be real, but as fate would have it, the gradual decline of his physicality [the weight loss and loss of motor skills] would start to war against my wishes and prayers for his recovery. I was in extreme denial of the current circumstances at the time. My mind would not allow for me to go into that dark place again: not as long as God's "breath of life" was still ebbing and flowing through him. I had been there before and did not want to go back.

Our father had passed when we were very young. I was caught off guard by his passing. To say that I was depressed would be an understatement. Destruction of my very inner being would be a more accurate depiction. I felt as though I had been killed and that I had died with my father.

James Tyrone Thomas was my big brother; after dad passed, something [miraculously] interesting happened to my brother's mentality. It underwent some sort of metamorphosis and he turned into a "father figure" to us [the younger siblings]. He began to treat me like his very own son. When I had to walk my eldest sister down the isle during her marriage ceremony, he bought me a brand new expensive suit [wanting me to look immaculate for the occasion]. After, I had graduated high school, I went on the college; after graduating college, I went into the workforce of corporate America and once again his personality changed; he went from father figure to best friend. I had moved from my hometown to a bigger city and going back to visit periodically, he was the number one constant and reason I looked forward to going back home, but now [a few decades later] it would come to this; he was wasting away and I couldn't do anything to help him.

All I knew was denial; it can't be happening. I refused to accept it; on one fateful day that I feared most, I got a call from my youngest sister. My brother's doctor had placed him on "hospice care." Everyone talked of much "doom and gloom" along the lines of:

"All we can do is keep him as comfortable as possible until 'The Day,' comes."
I still refused to acknowledge this; I even disputed their claims sighting,
"They call themselves 'Christians:' people of the faith, but as soon as the doctor gives his perception, their faith takes a nosedive and God's will for us to live victoriously goes out the window.

They have absolutely no faith!" I was angry over their submissive attitudes of his condition, but I did not overtly express my feelings to any of them.

However, I foolishly blamed them all for fighting [in spirit] against my brother's "will to live" because they were doubters: except for one of my nieces that understood him perhaps just as well as I and his second born son did. But I still refused to be defeated! I did not give up!"

Who are you going to believe, a doctor [of limited knowledge] or God Himself? I can recall going to see him in the facility. I had taken some days off just so I could go and have some "alone time" with him since everybody else would be at work. I honestly could not fathom why God would take him: while he was in his prime no doubt. But I continued to pray; after all, miracles do happen and maybe a miracle would be in store for us; I prayed for this miracle because as I explained to God, we truly need one. Perhaps this is exactly what it would take to get our family back on the healing path as a cohesive unit. Like many others, I came from a dysfunctional family environment and I attempted to petition God for a miracle [of healing] so that everyone would "see the light." A miracle would be just what the doctor ordered to get our divided family back on track. I had most certainly agreed to do my part. Is it truly possible to make a bargain with the Lord even as Gideon was said to have done so in the bible before he'd go on to fulfill his destiny? [Judges 6:17] Nevertheless, the time eventually came, and a relative contacted me early one morning and I was told that my brother "Transitioned."

I became numb. I immediately prepared to go home after informing my place of employment what I was told. On the way, all I could do was deny: thinking to myself, "This is an ultra-realistic lucid dream. When I get to my hometown, I will wake up and find myself back in bed in the city where I currently reside. I will realize that it was a long drawn out dream and that my brother was still alive and well. When I arrived to my hometown, I drove by the funeral home where his body was said to be lying in state. Several cars were parked out front and in the parking lot. I drove past it. I wanted to go in there alone. For whatever reason, I needed to go in alone. I waited for a few hours, and after seemingly everyone had left, I finally went in; I had felt anxiety before but the energy of this particular anxiety was not the typical type of nervousness that I was used to. As, I walked toward the open casket slowly drawing closer, I recognized him. There he lay: my brother, father, best friend (a true warrior). I say "warrior" because he was also a protector. Because of him, while growing up in a ratchet part of town, he helped my mother to keep me out of trouble and thwarted all manner of "would be" bullies from terrorizing me.

As I stood there viewing his body while wondering what the point of it all was, a demon would interrupt my visitation. It was an entity that had vexed me before and under the same circumstances as when my father had transitioned. I thought that I had exorcised this demon from my psyche some years ago, but I was gravely mistaken. It was the demon of depression. It had come back, and it came back with a vengeance.

Because this demon had [once again] reared its sinister head, I begin to question God's judgment; after all, we invested so much of our time, money, and lives [especially within the Christian church] and this is how it all comes to fruition? But there he lay [lifeless motionless]. He was gone. I never woke up from the dream that I deluded myself into thinking I was having. Speaking of dream, I will need to press the rewind button. Several days before my brother had transitioned, I said a prayer with intense emotion; I asked God to heal my brother. I don't recall how long I remained on my knees but I do recall being on bended knees to a point that I grew tired [even sleepy]. I went to bed that night [immediately after the prayer] and I had a dream:

Omega Mountain

In the dream, I had met my brother in what appeared to be an open field of some sort with no houses or buildings in site; he motioned with his hand for me to follow him, and he led me to what looked like a jagged pillar of rock that appeared to be infinitely tall. It was round: about 30ft circumference. Its color was like a light grayish translucent crystal. I asked him what was it, and he replied, "It's Omega Mountain, and I have been charged by God to climb to the top of it." I took another look at the structure and I noticed that he had no kind of climbing gear or equipment to assist him. Again, the sides of it were rough and jagged. It was covered with many gashes, cracks, and crevices that were barely wide enough to get the tips of the fingers and feet through.

The thing was so steep that it appeared as a straight vertical climb. But my brother [the warrior] appeared unmoved by the challenge even though the structure stretched so high that it disappeared into the clouds to where we couldn't tell exactly where it ended. He gave the thing a look of iron-willed determination and began to climb. Amazingly enough, he was able to grip the thing well enough to hoist himself upward. He scaled it as easily as a squirrel climbs a tree. He was very swift with the climb. A few times he lost his grip and slipped [falling a few feet downward] but managing to re-grasp and continue on up. I was amazed at his stamina. As he climbed, I was simultaneously lifted [levitating upward] to witness his feat. Also, as he climbed something miraculous began to occur right before my eyes. As he progressed upward, his strength and stamina were gradually increasing; likewise his physical appearance began to transform from one of sickness to restoration of health. After he reached a certain point, he appeared to be his healthy self again; however, he kept on climbing. It could be clearly seen that the higher he climbed, the stronger he got and his stamina was increasing as well, so instead of getting tired, he was actually climbing faster and faster: becoming increasingly energized.

Up he ascended into and finally above the clouds. Eventually, he made it to the very top. He stood upon a flat [3ft diameter circular] platform that was made of pure silver. It gleamed like a full moon on a clear and starry night. He stood there; gazing up at the sky and the heavens. All the while, I was hovering there in spirit. I was awe struck and was feeling very proud to be his brother. He looked at me in acknowledgment that the task was accomplished. It was at this point that the dream faded and I woke up. I did not go back to sleep right away. I stayed up for a while because I wanted to finish experiencing the feelings of joy and optimism that were surging through my emotions. After about 30 or 45 minutes, I drifted back off to sleep.

Two days later, I had another dream [a vision perhaps] because I don't have any recollection of feeling drowsy and dozing off to sleep, but the vision picked up where the previous dream left off. I was back in the sky, levitating beside Omega Mountain in spirit. My brother was standing on the gleaming silver platform [appearing in immaculate health and strength]. He stretched out both his arms to his sides and a golden cloak had materialized behind him; it seemed as though a pair of invisible hands were holding it as the cloak was draped about his shoulders from behind. I intuitively knew that the robe was made of 100% pure gold. However, it did not have the density of the metal, its texture was that of silk or satin and it draped easily around him. It glowed almost as bright as the sun to the point that I could barely look at it. He stretched his hands toward the sky and this nullified the glow to where I could look at it and see his face. Again, he looked at me for a moment, and from behind his shoulders, the invisible hands revealed a hood that was attached to the cloak. The hood was positioned over his head which prompted the cloak to glow like the sun once more. Like a flash of lighting that strikes down upon the earth, so did he make an exit [in an instant] like lightning that flashed upward into the heavens. He was gone [promoted to a more rarefied dimension of life than this one]. I hovered for a moment; however, I begin to slowly descend back toward the earth; somehow, I found myself back in my bed at home [still wide awake].

Initially, I thought the 1st dream meant that he would not only fight the good fight but would win in convincing fashion because in real life, he was a fighter and a true winner; if anybody could beat something like this, he'd be the one; he'd be the miracle man with a mighty testimony to give. I thought that the dream meant that he'd make a full recovery and life would eventually return back to normal, but as you may have already guessed, it meant something entirely different. But at the same time, it was revealed to me that it meant something much more wonderful than this earth-life could ever offer. It meant that a place was prepared for him: a position to occupy and a platform to stand upon within the next level of existence. I was totally content with this revelation; I felt a sense of bliss knowing that my brother had made it to the other side and that he was cloaked in a golden robe of God's glory. I even felt a little envious afterward.

After the second dream [vision], so many other realizations started pouring into my mind, and all that I can say is that the revelations did not come from me; in a way, I had received the miracle that I was praying for all along. The very first and obvious one is that, my brother had truly transitioned into another world: a greater level of existence that I have yet to experience. He is still alive and well! In spite of all that happened [including my questioning of God's judgment] I felt at peace. I was able to accept God's greater level of wisdom and His will for my brother's ascension into the heavens. In an instant, the demon [depression] had been banished, and the most impactfull realization had to do with this earth life and the fact that it isn't a permanent existence for any human being. We will all have to transition to another level of life. Therefore, it is better not to cling mentally to our loved ones because we cannot avoid the inevitable, so I realized that I had to let my brother move on. I was only hurting myself by clinging to him. God revealed to me that I was being selfish because my subconscious mentality was "What's going to become of me and my life now that my brother has moved on?"

This life isn't forever and it is always in a state of constant change. Anything that changes is not permanent, and if it is not permanent, then it has to be an illusion [a dream]. Perhaps the most significant revelation was that I am the one dreaming; my brother was called upon to awaken from the dream [of this drudgery that we call earth-life] and I have yet to do so. And I also consciously realized that I was being unfair to him by wanting him to stay behind with me; his spiritual evolution and his journey toward greater life would be denied by wishing for him to remain here [in this dream]. It is now January 16, 2019, and I am still dreaming within this impermanent life; perhaps you are too; perhaps your loved one has awakened from this "dream" that we believe to be real life, and like my brother and your beloved, perhaps God will eventually call upon the rest of us to wake up. And perhaps we shall all celebrate together, even as the angels in heaven rejoice.

Nevertheless, I have come to a realistic conviction that with "faith in God" all things are possible. I have come to a full realization that as sure as we are here in this world, Something and Someone within, outside, and beyond this world set it all up and put us all here; therefore, reality is not limited to this world and neither are we, and we should be grateful that our loved ones have ascended to a better, nobler, and much grander existence than this one. We should rejoice that eventually so will we.

Behold, I shew you a mystery; We shall not all sleep, but we shall all be changed, In a moment, in the twinkling of an eye, at the last trump: for the trumpet shall sound, and the dead shall be raised incorruptible, and we shall be changed.

[1 Corinthians 15:51-52 KJV]

Let Go And Let God

We must make up our minds to "let go." God won't change our minds for us; this is up to us. It is up to us to come to a place of certainty that gives God the permission He requires to act on our behalf and answer our prayers. We must truly be transformed, [renewed of the mind]. The dilemma is that we try to forcefully inspire and motivate ourselves with the wrong methodology. We try to think positively or constructively about our loved one's situation but more times than not, success is short lived. Having to struggle against thoughts of negativity with forced thoughts of positivity and all the while the health and condition of our beloved seems to bc getting worse will usually result in disappointment. At that point, we feel that we don't even want to think about the situation and that is exactly what we must do [or not do]. Thinking is the wrong solution. The way to mental healing and mind renewal which restores faith is moreso about "not thinking" as opposed to "thinking." Not thinking about the situation and just being aware of the situation is the only way to help matters. If you are thinking about the situation and you have a negative mindset, then your spirit is mentally absorbed. And your mind was never meant to be a dwelling place for you spirit. Your spirit is meant to be free from the constraints of the mind. If your spirit gets absorbed into your mind in whatever capacity, it becomes imprisoned, anxious, and afraid. All that can come of it is suffering: mental anguish, faithless doubt, and emotional pain. While inside the mind, your spirit will latch onto memories that it mistakes for real life. If you allow your spirit to be lulled into the confines of the mind the only places it can go is into the [terrifying] unconscious darkness or the house of your mental memory. While absorbed within the mind, the spirit fears the unconscious darkness which is why it resorts to using memories for assurance of life. To the spirit that dwells within the narrow parameters of its very own mind, it has no other choice but to think that memories of past events are reality. Everywhere it ventures [while absorbed in the mind] it encounters old ghosts and demons that tend to haunt and torment it. While mentally absorbed, it even uses past memories to construct new [but illusory] realities that never even happened in real life.

This is where we tend to make our greatest errors when attempting to deal with the death of a loved one. You must understand what is happening to you by consciously observing your situation. Do you realize that whenever you conjure up a memory of a deceased loved one, often times the mind tends to create a new memory out of an old one which simultaneously reinforces your grief?

For instance, when you recollect a memory of a your beloved, a thought such as "She should have been here to see and experience this with me," may result; the mind typically visualizes a picture of the loved one being there to experience what you are experiencing in that moment. However, reality shows you that the loved one is not there. Therefore the thought of the loved one being there gets intermingled with the truth that she is not. The mind unconsciously processes both ideas as if they are real. The two ideas conflict and the mental confusion that results because of the contrary ideas tend to delay or prevent healing all together. The mourning processes hence may become traumatic as opposed to healing. Your loved one would never want you to suffer on his or her behalf when you could be experiencing joy instead.

Again, you may bo creating unrealistic realities [stemming from sheer memory] which your mind takes as valid memories from previous memories, and as these memories continue to multiply and occupy the mind, it could very well be possible that you never get over the passage of your loved one who has moved on and into the kingdom of God.

This is called "mental clinging" [because of "mental clinging" some people even become so fixated that they never get over the fact that a loved one has advanced to the next level of life]. Often times you hear about someone that never remarries or form new relationships and in some cases herein lies the reason why; they cling to the past and in their own way, they continue to create [illusory present moments] with memories of the past and recollections of former "good times" that were shared; there is a subconscious notion that the loved one must be kept alive and well and that it is their responsibility to keep them in a state of present time existence with the faculty of memory: they unknowingly usurp the job that God Himself does for us all.

Three hundred years from now, even the griever will be forgotten [by people], but God can never forget anyone. We must be careful to not place ourselves in a state of self-torment by misuse of the memory. Understand that this [type of grieving (mentally clinging)] is a potentially unhealthy practice; whereas the mourning process was meant to get over the pain of a loved one's absence [because mourning should be an act of letting go], it may be being used to increase and perpetuate grief because of "holding on." "Mindful mourning" is the answer. There is a big push in both spiritual and religious organizations of the concept of being "mindful." The teaching of "Spiritology" calls it "self awareness" or simply "awareness." What this means is that you must consciously grieve or mourn the death of your beloved which equates to letting them go; you are aware of the grief and pain [which is caused by the mental disconnection] that you feel as opposed to being mentally absorbed into the pain. And again, it is the mental absorption [being consciously fixed in the mind's memory and unconscious regions] that empowers and increases the grief; all memories are illusions, and there is an illusion that the loved one is still alive and well which clashes with the reality that they are no longer on this earthly plain. You cling to them in the mind because you want them to be "here," but when you walk into that vacant room, reality reminds you that they have moved on. It is the clashing of the illusion with the reality that causes inner pain and suffering. The grief does not wane; it tends to get more powerful as you process it this way; the outside world of reality gradually ceases to exist for you and depression could be the very next stage.

When you grieve in a conscious manner, you let go [psychologically] of the loved one. This is what you must do. It does not mean that you cease to remember, but you recall in the right way [the spiritual way]. You get yourself outside of the prison cell that you have created within your mind and into the open space of the kingdom of God which is where your loved one now dwells. When you do it this way, you cease to struggle with the [sometimes agonizing] processes of remembering your loved one and consciously realize [in a state of total joy] that they are still with you. You are actually letting go of the "initial painful mental ego disconnect" that happened when your loved one passed on, so that you may spiritually reconnect from a much higher realistic and Greater Perspective.

Many believe that without clinging to loved ones in this psychological manner, their spirits are completely freed to enter into the kingdom of God in full capacity; they are no longer being anchored to this troubled world. And if you let go, if you become fully conscious [mindful], you too enter into God's Kingdom; all the while you still don the body of physicality; looked at in this light, you are not only in God's Kingdom and enveloped by the love of God, you are also there with your loved one [sharing an elevated kind of reality that is outside of the constrictions of your mind and also above and beyond this world] and you both share that state of joy and the "peace that passeth all understanding" together. You will know that your loved one is alright and best of all, you know that your very own soul is safe and secure [in this world and will be so in the world to come]. And although the five sensory perceptions are not necessarily there as it relates to the body and mind connections with your beloved, there is a mental to spiritual perception [which is God's ultimate perception] that takes its place [it is a mind to spirit sensory perception]. You are hence reconnected to God in spirit and that connection is what connects you to your loved one and you finally realize that he or she is truly in Heaven [and so are you].

In ancient times, certain cultures would perform "last rites:" funeral ceremonies. The ceremonies were meant to be celebratory of the loved one's passage to a greater level of life. After the celebration, the physical body would be put on a cot in a boat; the boat would have flammable combustible materials underneath and around the body. The inner portions of the boat would be ignited with fire and sent to drift off into the sea or lake. It was a supreme act of letting go; they understood that the body was the vessel and that the vessel is temporal; keeping the vessel around only served to anchor the loved one to this earthly existence, so the loved one had to be fully freed in this manner.

The ancients were truly wise to reality, and they knew that their loved one was in a much better place; there was no mental clinging because they understood completely that no one is ever truly gone or lost. You can have that very same understanding beyond "intellectual knowing" which is completely different from "conscious knowing."

You must keep in mind that God has a mind and a memory too that not only houses your memory but the memories of every human being on the face of the earth [including those that have come and gone]. Not only that, but God also has a consciousness that houses your consciousness and the consciousness of all people who are here and those that we perceive [with the 5 senses] who have moved on. Now you can see exactly why in the mind and eyes of God they are still here. And if you get outside of your limited mindspace and into the open arena of God's mind and consciousness, you spiritually are reunited with your loved one as opposed to selfishly mentally clinging.

You don't have to cling to your loved one by way of tormenting memories of what once was and what could have been. Instead of clinging to them which equates to keeping them in this unforgiving world and in a state of suffering, why not let them go? As you do so, you enter into the kingdom of God with them. You can be together forever and God will wipe away all of your tears because suffering will at long last become as a vague distant memory because death itself will no longer be understood as an "ultimate reality." [Revelation 21: 4-6]

There are friends who pretend to be friends, but there is a friend who sticks closer than a brother. [Proverbs 18:24 The Living Bible (Paraphrased) Self-Help Edition]

This book is dedicated to the conscious memory of James Tyrone Thomas Sr., A beloved father, friend, and brother.

The act of grieving is a process that just about everyone will eventually be made to endure. There are five commonly recognizable stages to the grieving process that are as follows:

Denial
Anger
Bargaining
Depression
Acceptance

The grieving individual may not necessarily experience all of them or even experience them in the exact same order; nevertheless, I hope that my personal experience may serve to shed some light upon your very own, and I pray that you [the reader] will be made to experience the final stage that is "Acceptance." Acceptance of the natural order of existence is crucial not only to your healing, but it is also crucial to your loved one's unimpeded transition.

May the grace of God calm your mind and comfort your heart always and forever.

Dario Thomas

Related Recommended Reading by Dario Thomas:

"In Every Life Some Rain Must Fall: The Power of Spiritology VI"

This book takes an in-depth look at the phenomenon of "depression," what it is and how it can be conquered once and for all.

"The Power of Spiritology I"
This book will show the reader the exact difference between "conscious awareness" and "mental absorption" first by giving accurate "down to earth" definitions and descriptions along with an easily applicable but powerfully effective methodology of implementing the process of "awareness." The reader will be made to understand the difference between being conscious of grief as opposed to being absorbed in it, and how to maintain a level of consciousness so that the healing of grief occurs. That and much more is covered in this work.

"The Power of Prayer: Every Thought A Prayer"
Often times we tend to get disappointed after praying because we don't get what we pray for; some of us even question God as I doubted Him

when my brother's earth-life was hanging in the balance. Nevertheless, when one prays, the prayer must be done at the level of consciousness; prayer must not be done on the platform of the mind where mental opposition resides; otherwise thoughts of doubt and all other manner of negativity can creep into our minds that diffuse or work against the prayers we attempt to offer up to God. As the messiah said, "Those that worship God must do so in truth and in spirit," [John 4:24] so must we pray in the same way. This book will show you how to accomplish this.

"As A Man Believeth"
This book gives the reader an easy applicable way to examine up close and personal his very own belief systems. It shows how to identify those beliefs that hinder and the ones that enhance life by becoming aware of them by watching them in action: as they tell and write out his life's story by way of the unfolding scenarios and circumstances that he encounters and deals with in real-time reality. It also shows how to dispense with limiting beliefs and amplify beliefs that are empowering.

Other Books By The Author:

The Power of Spiritology II, I Am the Devil
This book is a must (especially if you are a Christian). It will give you great insight and understanding into the nature of the devil. You will be made to understand (at deeper levels of mind) that you are never at Satan's mercy. Finally, you will be able to defeat him once and for all by casting him [and his voice that is the voice of contradiction to the Spirit] out of your mind once and for all.

The Power of Spiritology III, Let Go Your Ego

The Power of Spiritology IV, Exercises for Spiritual Growth

The Art of Spiritual Listening

The Power of Alchemy, The Higher Science of God

All Books Are Available For Purchase At Amazon.com